D1585953

OUT OF THE AIR

IE I   ERSITY OF
          STE'

Also by Jeffrey Wainwright from Carcanet

Selected Poems
The Red-Headed Pupil

Jeffrey Wainwright

OUT OF THE AIR

CARCANET

First published in 1999 by
Carcanet Press Limited
4th Floor, Conavon Court
12-16 Blackfriars Street
Manchester M3 5BQ

A CIP catalogue record for this book
is available from the British Library
ISBN 1 85754 415 3

The publisher acknowledges financial assistance
from the Arts Council of England

Set in 10pt Garamond Simoncini by Bryan Williamson, Frome
Printed and bound in England by SRP Ltd, Exeter

for my Mother

and in memory of my Father

Acknowledgements and Notes

'Out of the Air' appeared first in the *Times Literary Supplement*,
9 August 1996.
'The Apparent Colonnades' was broadcast on BBC Radio 3 in 1996
and published in *PN Review* 115, 1997.
'Anne's Shells' has appeared in *Grand Street*, New York.

Thanks for reading, advice and support to Jon Glover, Avril Horner,
and to the Department of English at The Manchester Metropolitan
University. Especial thanks to Michael Schmidt and Judith
Wainwright.

*

'Broken Symmetry', '. . . that the whole universe . . . etc', Paul
Claudel in *The Correspondence 1899-1926 between Paul Claudel and
André Gide*, trans John Russell, London: Secker & Warburg, 1952,
pp. 53-4.

'Form Law Order Sequence' draws upon Henry Adams (1838-1918),
specifically *The Education of Henry Adams* (1907; 1918), Ch XV,
'Darwinism'.

'The Humane House' draws upon Henry David Thoreau (1817-62),
specifically 'The Beach', Ch IV, and 'The Sea and the Desert', Ch IX
of *Cape Cod*, Thomas Y. Crowell, New York, 1961, Apollo edition,
New York, 1966. The epigraph is from his *Walden, or Life in the
Woods* (1854), 'Economy', Holt Rinehart and Winston, New York,
1963, p.18.

'The Apparent Colonnades' takes its title from a painting by Michael
Andrews in The Whitworth Art Gallery, Manchester.

' "War Poems": Six Pieces', 'The dead are unhappy enough . . . etc',
Marguerite Long, pianist and widow of Captain Joseph de Marliave,
who gave the first performance of Maurice Ravel's *Le Tombeau de
Couperin*, a work dedicated to her first husband and five other
friends of Ravel killed in the 1914-18 War. Quoted in Gerald Larner,
Maurice Ravel, London: Phaidon, 1966, p.164.

7

Contents

9

Out of the Air
i.m. Sidney Wainwright 1910-1995

Every moment is exhalation, an appointed
        sacrifice, like that
poured upon the ground saying, this is what we are, no more,

thus are we expended, by reflex, just as, from that smack on,
        we draw the fraction
that we need from what swathes us now

and oxidize divinity, put what should go on forever
        to our use,
worked through every track and gully of this catacomb,

changed, as we perform our repetitions,
        into our change,
we beings as nearly metabolous as the fly:

in the lover's lightest rise and fall asleep,
        our flustered age,
within the infant's sigh a rapturous somersault.

*

Until, *de facto*, the air does not go on,
that until arrives,
– *my last breath, with my dying breath* –

and I am able to bring in no more, include,
embrace no more,
put the last roughed centilitres aside

barely drawn upon, pushed away, defrayed –
puff . . . puff . . . it goes
and there is no fellow can replace it,

and I am what I was, untouched, unentered,
the merest solidity,
insufficient, what is called clay.

*

Out of all the whorls and eddies of air –
               part of it sustenance
contributed by kale and dock leaves, anciently

the blue-green algae of bacterial seas, some of it
               let out of the bag
to white out Montcalm or the western cwm –

comes the draught in Men's Medical this afternoon,
               and all the fussing
with the window-pole, especially for the man across

who sits crinkled in foil, coddled in moon-boots
               against his enemy,
which is yet also the old man's friend,

busy, and healthily scented here, always on hand
               to be snipped
and walleted in the shallowing lung,

until nothing can be done with it,
               until it pauses
at the lips, and passes, unexchanged

*

13

Out of the amorphousness of air, particulars,
nothing crystalline,
(and there are no 'instances') but

such as: *You are my heart's delight*
And where you ar – rre
I long to be – mac over the shoulder,

trilby pushed back – that was the style
but that was the man –
whistling along the street, hope springing

eternal, as you used to say, usually
satirically, defending
yourself against fortune too by exactitudes:

the slivers of tape on the radio dial,
the inks and keys
of clerking, the mortgage on the dot,

nothing done anyhow, till now –

. . .   . . .
O that you could catch your breath again

*

Nearly every night I meet you
              in the underworld of dream.
You are waiting impatiently upon the lawn

or in the porch against the leaded glass.
              'Yes, I have come at last.
Yes, you did all you could,' 'Yes, enough'.

Now, with every policy and scrap of adding-up in place,
              from where you are,
you who felt the century so much closer to,

say, is there a future that you can foretell?
              Some instruction?
Is there another library you can take me to?

You do not speak and cannot stay –
              the porch is cold
even for stoics – here backs always turn eventually.

Which is why I keep your razor as it is,
              your stubble still inside,
a tiny, capsuled drift – I cannot let it go.

It seems the last of you, but out of it
              I change you back
and see you in a cloudless pool recovering length

by length that perfect crawl you never could quite teach
              the shiverer, who is,
even so, left to himself, the better for your breath.

Ghosts

The world – I mean the mind – is full of ghosts:
The husband, pronounced dead but palpable enough in bed
To hug, returns in bandages, his arm in a sling,
Beating at the back-door to be let in.

The world – I mean the universe – is full of itself:
Angles and relativities, compressions of the deep,
The steady tread of light bumping the earth, the waves
An abstraction of the nearly changeless sea.

Sometimes it can seem we are anywhere but here
Even though the ground insists upon it,
Stamps the soles of our feet to interrupt
How we would naturally be which is floating or falling.

All the dead want

All the dead want of us is praise.

Or so we think.

Though words are crabby and coagulate,
embarrass us
                       easier they are
than incontinence and phlegm.

We incise pure letters.
We walk to visit them.
We build them little towns, where,
when we have locked them in at night,
we fancy they might nod to one another,
sit on stools and knit
or furrow over football pools.

And we will speak well.
We will speak well.

But beforehand, blessèd are those by them in their desperation,
and that is bodily.
Blessèd are the hurried launderers
who lay on hands.

Doing Philosophy

Let the philosopher enjoy his dying –
It is his true profession after all: what he is
Readied for; it is the only knowledge and it's left till last.
Does it matter there is no speaking it?

Let the philosopher enjoy his dying
Despite the body's renitence at being
Put aside, its soaking of the sheets,
Its lamp-lace frailty, its brain in clouds.

For what could it do, this body, in its pomp?
Was there anything it could say it knew?
Any jealousy it could deny itself?
What was that beauty it stumbled on

But musk and appetite, like the bed on summer
Afternoons, even less complex than the purposes of flies
Haunting the will to fix them in their sorts?
Left to his mind he would not love you, dear.

So let the philosopher enjoy his dying –
Though there will be no thinking then
He knows we are a thought, not hapless bleeding.
It must not matter there is no speaking it.

The Slow Breathers

The slow breathers,
the saltie in Queensland
the tortoise on the lawn
live longer,

keep the gristly inside bark
of themselves
the less abraded,
the lacy sponge of the lung

in shape, admit errors more rarely –
the granulation under the eyelids
thus slowed down
for instance –

altogether roll more easily
with the regulation roughing-up
from oxygen, that happy, happy
synthesis of long, long ago.

Broken Symmetry

'... that the whole universe is never still for a moment ...
everything is movement ...'

Yes, everywhere, arcs in description –
San Lorenzo's tears of fire wiped once across the sky –
and beyond them the vermiculate heavens
whose nonetheless stolid beams
endure their march-time loneliness,
dispatch their resonances,
towards or away from us,
afoot with hares in the sallows, moles in the turf,
on one of the possible paths –
perhaps 'classical', perhaps not –
but in truth much as they seem,
else how would we watchers, who feel our time daily,
be here to spot the rates of change of rates of change?

*

As of the pool's aspiration always to stillness;
the blood's spiral stopping in your veins,
its cells no longer performing their virtuoso squeeze
through but settling for gravity,
the contusion gathering along the line of the bed;
though in your drying is still movement, moisture
only slowly given up to the desired default towards symmetry,
the pool's plane expanding its recovery from brokenness,
its grasp to have everything identified, singular,
to absorb the cut flowers in the vase
and the open Testament
into its peace.

Outside, the ranks of daffodils are racing.
Nightly he floats his clay-white face up to her.

Take me by the hand

Take me, someone, by the hand,
Lead me down the hill,
Put me by the fire's side.

The buses strain and skid on the cinders.
We totter and slip upwards.
My fingers, screwed tight,
Whiten from the tip.

Take me, someone, by the hand,
Lead me down the hill,
Put me by the fire's side.

Anne's Shells
i.m. Anne Alexander Davidson 1937-1994

I say your shells though they are not really so.
I scooped them randomly from the beach
Plus a piece of blue crabber's twine as something
Of the place to tie you stubbornly in mind.

Placing them on a book page, I set to learning
Of their lives – identifying the teeth sockets
Studded on the hinge, the muscle scar of attachment
Where the body lay, its sinus sipping its goodness from the deeps.

This one will take so strong a tap it seems it is with us still:
Good morning brother scallop shell, kinned in calcium,
Self-assembled from the slosh we are,
Hard palate, hard ridge, bone of each other's bone,

Both so sturdy from siphoning our own patch of helpful universe,
The accumulate of a system whose glory is a finger nail,
The brick-by-brick, flight-by-flight of limes,
You particularised by the ocean's shrug, I likewise by the working air.

But we are not gold and time has already had some way with you.
At length what we will both together be is calx:
I, municipal tilth, you by incidentals
Abraded and raised elsewhere in the firmament,

And nothing can say this is just a different way to be,
That we can be content to be amalgamate again,
Spiting complexity, mindless in Poseidon's facelessness,
Gratefully lost in a shudder from Saturn's storms.

No, Anne, that is not where you are now,
Nor strolling in the gallery of forms, however configured
As Love, Justice, even Music, not gathered by rivers,
Not harmonical upon the prairies of the blest.

25

Nothing is better than to live – *inter homines esse* –
That is the synonym that stirs the ghosts to walk,
Makes the dead stretch out their thin arms to us
When we visit them – how could we beat them off?

They know what they are missing and that is it.
Living in the common sense of grief the fact is
You are not, no matter how much you visit by dreams,
Seem by surprise to be there at the table

And seem talkable to – you are not –
inter homines esse desinere – ceased to be among –
Desinent, to meet another word spiralling from
The gastropod into your absence

As, *estuarine, byssus, sessile, evaporite.*
Your shells lead me along a shoreline of information:
A few pages back, before there was Ynyslas,
Before there was Wales, out of the great swoosh

Of 'marine transgression', the taking and shaking of the earth
By chalky seas, then 'grave majestic Tethys' stepping back
As the Atlantic newly opens, building such details as
The Blue Point Oyster, *Crassotrea Virginica,*

And by the flick of a word stem I nudge you again
In what was called the Goodness of Virginia
Whose trees rained such rich and pleasant gums,
Which furnished such several kinds of flax,

The wapeih found so good for sores and wounds,
So many apothecary drugs, and vegetables 'far better
Than our English peas'. Out of all this came the health
And sprightliness by which you could turn cartwheels

In Edinburgh drawing-rooms – Summers at the shore,
The car loaded with the sunshines of America,
Passing Yorktown, Newport News – maybe the *Nautilus* out there
Test-diving in the roads – across the Chesapeake

26

And up 13, Cape Charles, Birdsnest, Jamesville,
Accomac, Modest Town, Temperanceville,
Chincoteague, the sand between your toes
On the beach where you are now sort of home again,

A modicum of outlandish, nearly-foreign calcite
Upon your National Seashore: 'Look for me
Beneath your feet' (your National Bard) – but does silicate, even
That anchoring beach-grass, truly show there is no death?

How many wake each morning, the wallpaper
Aged another night about them, and wish themselves
No more than the shell's abrasion,
At least no more than mechanical lingula,

The inarticulate, burrowed into the tidal flat,
Digesting the brack in as straightforward
A life as there has ever been,
Gentler by far than the sky waiting above the counterpane?

But this will not do. Though sand does get everywhere,
Into hair, socks, peanut-butter,
This is to be as fixed on the physical as when
In that summer in Galloway we could think of nothing

But midges, the children puffy, red and miserable,
All of us bitten to death,
And none of us philosopher enough to abide
The next itch wherever it was coming from.

Surely that seven-league stride – the mosses'
Maiden foothold, the worts breathing their first
To sweeten the gases into air, the millipedes'
Bronchial march – brought across the beach

Some spore that will eventually propose a mind
That can be comfortable with where it finds itself,
Undismayed that the body breaks,
Unimpressed by word of something liftable from its bones?

27

It would be so calm because so certain of the laws,
The power of lines and angles true everywhere,
Forever, which does not change and does not speak
And cannot be coloured in as the urgent angel –

Oh his golden head, his outstretched arm! –
Telling her how much better things would be.
At last will the universe have crackled,
But only to show how we are in motion and where

Exactly – 'There, there' – the indifference
Welcome because unwelcoming: we need not reply.
Summarised, sessile at last,
We could wait for that amen – could we?

But if that still is facelessness, and unbearable,
Watch Anne, and learn to bob on the unbroken deep.
Nothing about this will help us fathom it,
But learning to strike out upon it is our own storybook:

On pins, on tip-toe, until that moment –
The child races home to tell –
Both feet are off the bottom and holding on to
Nothing, frantic, grinning, paddling – but look, look!

To teach swimming is to be at work at life.
Here is the space I am, here is the time,
From where I will be in Lesson 1, standing on the side,
To breasting the swells running the creek towards me.

To teach a simple pleasure, a simple practice,
So someone can turn their back upon the deep
And float in the sun is an act of reason:
The space about me will be different, time will change.

In the pool or that miniature cove of the Pacific,
We see the world is not a hospital, nor an inn,
No kind of stop-over. To live is not to sit frozen
Before the fire or the blank of the fading wall.

Every stroke is an act, braving the trench
Below, and to show how to half-way master it
Brings joy to the tremulous child,
Goose-pimpled and improbable not an hour ago.

The gift is swimming, for the child one perfect point
Of alteration, a capability in the outside,
A splashy gait which is part of just themselves,
Some moments incommunicado, life-saving, learnt by exchange.

So, having lost another sock, on from Pwll Nofio they go,
Pellagra and the buboes long since conquered in their name,
To take their place in marriages
That mostly work, to stand behind counters,

To pick up the brochures yearly and do their sums,
Be hushed by news of sudden death,
Love their children, spoil their children,
Be damped into depression's anthracites,

Make a go of fitted kitchens, TV Repair, nursery teaching,
To be a fusilier as he always dreamed –
The first lost from his class, on the News it was –
Adopt a little Chinese girl who's doing fine,

Stop, unnerved, at the ward's overlapping doors,
Leave home, just change entirely,
Settle down at last – shorter than she'd hoped, and spotty –
Shoulder Oxfam's sacks and tallies in Libreville.

What are we doing, some of us, tonight, 8.7.97?
In the USA it is Janet's birthday
And the party must have started early
For John can't reach her on the phone.

He and we are eating an ordinary supper,
Save for the red wine, not usual for a Tuesday,
And – decent folk of Temperanceville as we are –
We make the jokes about that which have become traditional.

29

Ghana is not of course the place, if challenged,
I would now muster up in mind and it is there
Tom – after a day at work for water,
Up to his waist in a real *vita activa* – will be sleeping now.

Then John, the younger John, of whom his father says
'Who knows?' but no news means ok, will have left
His sleepless systems idling, but maybe finds himself
With a bucket under the eaves – freak storms in London apparently.

And at the neck of Chesapeake and Delaware,
Your father is still eager with the *New York Times*,
Your mother, white hair and her own mind still taut,
Gazes on the summer green as on that unseasonal snow.

And so on, across the ripple of all of 'us' –
Defined as who knew you – now cruelly going on,
Inhabiting these moments like the clatter of dishes does,
And the horn practice just starting now along the street.

Stoic

We are your friends, and, of course, willingly so,
Easily, because we love you for the quiddit
That is knowing you, all sorts of chewing-over:
What is surplus value? Could it be that additives

Are sedging the brains of kids these days? –
Look how they scream in checkout queues;
And cricket; and the running jokes of thirty years
I could not raise a laugh with here.

But when you've gone for the bus, and a minute later
I see it go by and wave, you look accidentally
Past me because already you are back
In what must be called your solitude.

Then, in a snatch of a waking dream,
Where the two of us are side by side in bed,
I see you outside, down the slope by the lakeshore,
The white of your cigarette in the dawn light.

This is, though you would not want to push the word,
Loneliness, which must be spoken to: 'I am at odds
With how the world and its courses have dealt with me.
Somehow with its indifference I must be reconciled.'

Ratio

the clocks of coal
the clocks of lime
the clocks of sandstone, shale and schist

'What time is it?' she asked

                                        They filled the house

with Bach: *'Let us not divide . . .'*

                                        the welter of winds and waters

in their fractions

                  her slowed step

                        a few paces from the car

some pipework bustles in the wall

                              a winter fly stutters by the window-pane

a phone answered quickly

                                      Where

is the denominator to recognise the consonance

of these intervals?

The Apparent Colonnades

1

Across the red cliff, dotted in, stand the apparent colonnades.
The sun will know the truth of them,
How far they resemble basilicas or market-halls,
Whether an entrance might be concealed.
He will march through them fearlessly, knowing there is nothing
                                behind him, not even blackness,
For he never sees darkness,
Cannot conceive of shadow,
Has no need even to imagine a smudge.
He is where all such knowledge starts,
Semplice lume, somma luce,
All hues in all proportions,
Undivided and in no need of difference to see.

2

Compare the painter's muddle:
'The *apparent* colonnades';
The locomotive all at sea with steam and dusk, the firebox over-
                              dramatised upon the viaduct;
The fancy that at evening the walls and trees themselves dispense the
                                                            light;
That it was the artist's intuition that devised the still trapezist's
                                          shadow on the wall.

Nor, given a subject, can any two of them agree just how it was:
Christ lies pinkly, greyly, austerely blind;
Christ poses spotlit among the shavings, like a five-year old at a party;
Christ folded into linen in so many different tombs;
Christ scrawny, ragg'd with spines, observing his armpit;
Christ in a dab of shadow, often a full poultice-paste of blackness, light
  only allowed across his brow and the buffed shine of the black cuirass.
Somewhere, perhaps, a Christ sorry for himself, hiding under a table,
                                          a little boy after all.

And, especially in executions, so much obscurity:
Who is this dark-furred judge presiding?
Who is this 'dead father', as wasted as by months entombed, roped
                                                      to a tree?
Does the curly-headed archer – foreground illuminated –
Think his shaded mark is Death itself?

3

But sunny Apollo falls upon all this evenly,
No sunkenness or hollowing,
Everything is there.
Thus he can pick out the unfinished hands of he who pulled a knife
$\qquad\qquad\qquad\qquad\qquad\qquad\qquad$ in a robbery,
He who shot the man kneeling by the safe in *Kwik-Save*.
To that curve in the brain, the sickle shape of *vanitas* within the
$\qquad\qquad\qquad\qquad\qquad\qquad$ male-factor's skull he penetrates,
And thus reassures the People's headsman,
Puts the felon to rasp brazilwood,
To the rope, the bull's pizzle, the hundred lashes,
To work the drowning cell –
Burning and grim he is, his eyes a domino of flame –
And so she should go down and dangle,
Peroxide bitch!

37

4

An argument should be approaching now
But only a cadence comes.
It rises to conclude that
We are all of us like painters and their kin,
All inside the light,
Only knowing what we know by darkness
And its feats of shadow.

It is a weak procedure for showing ourselves the world,
And still more for drawing out of our own heads such things as
Justice –
That which we know we need but don't know the look of
Beyond that it is everything that is due,
And is strife, not vision (if we are tough enough),
And its every smudge is Tragedy,
All that is spilt, that could not become capable of solution, what
makes us gasp, terror –
Though we can turn that to advantage and wangle beauty from it,
The *chiaroscuro* Apollo has not a glimmer of,
A mood where we can ponder
Who is the cross-hatched old man sagging at the mark?
Does the dark-furred judge doubt he knows the facts?
Is the curly-headed archer praying 'Christ, Apollo, tell me this is
right!'?

And what of the boy beneath the table
Who fears both the friends outside and friendlessness,
Fears both any kind of love and this solitude he seeks,
Who wants to be away, untouched in there, his own ragged splotch
of life
Untamed by wisdom as she is practised?
He pulls the cloth down against the shiny afternoon,
Thinking he can keep it out, that he will not be seen,
And he is not.

He shoots the man he has kneeling by the safe in *Kwik-Save*.
This is where the argument and poem end.
How he would love simple, perfect light.

38

The Humane House

'It is desirable that a man be clad so simply
that he can lay his hands on himself in the dark.'

At a knot-hole, looking inwards, ocean, land,
Beach and sky, everything outer, behind us,
If we watch faithfully we will see at length
Some wandering beam dawdle upon a shape within.

Thus Thoreau, walking one day along the Cape,
Beside the sea that comes ashore so
Indecorously, retreated from its inhuman tucks and turns
To seek and even enter that 'long-wished-for insight'.

So creased is his eye-socket against the grain,
He must believe that it is there: rolled round,
Concealed in the metaphor of a house for castaways,
Waiting on a patch of lamp-glass, the scratch on a tin plate.

Unless, as he watched, he felt a sand-grain cross his eyeball,
Sensed as he stood the contrition of all those
Unfleshed carcasses drive under the door and past the window-frame,
Filling the house, chasing apart the tinier and tinier

Crossways of light until they are holed up
And drowning between the close-fit slopes of sand,
Suffocated beneath a run-away now of beach and sky,
The last of light dragged first from our dwarfish sun

Then from the millions of suns still left,
Hoppered through the chimney, sucked through clapboard cracks
To be so crushed there will truly be nothing to see
And not even blackness to attend do.

What he had sought in an eventual gleam inside
Were 'the very bowels of mercy':
Some magnanimity, trust, practicality,
A gift of straw to make a fire out of the wind.

39

Instead he finds himself bystander at this last
Cataract of being. He unclasps his eye,
Wedges his feet in the sand and feels for his shirt-button
And a nubbin of flesh 'twixt thumb and forefinger.

Form Law Order Sequence

Away from the tide's tucks and turns, educated Henry,
Looking out above his ghostly Shropshire sea
Wanted something that would speak from the shale
And suggest a sequence where he, who 'had just helped

Waste a million lives, more or less', could with his pen-strokes
Belong. He tapped and found the trilobites,
Impressive, thoughtful starfish 'whose kindly descendants'
He had back-flipped among in Quincy Bay,

An American in search of a father better than his father
And whom he could exceed towards perfection everlasting
Whether having come by lungs or gills no matter.
But it is only Change, he thought: at best the betterment

Of gooseberries, plumper, hairless, pinker at the heart;
Coal: power: the mortar hidden in peach-trees:
The sharp-shooter's last sleep. And he ceased to care
Whether the truth were true, putting it as flat as that.

41

*

Eterni Angelette

Gaitano instructs,
but transliterating an unfamiliar hand
or mishearing the phonics,
the mason bequeathes disagreement,
'Eterni Angelette',
a stricken nicety,
to weather and all time:

Angelina giorni 7

and within twelve days

Mariuccia giorni 18

perhaps of some common fever
or tramway accident,
barely into the new century
the new country
this New South Wales.

So the pain cuts

nostre cuore
nostre figlie

who must never know the blight
of the chestnut trees
drying in the valleys,
or the white fields of Calabria

or wherever,

or the mattress dragging over the cartwheels,
never have that as *memorìa,*

45

but stand on tip-toe on this cliff-top,
in fresh space,
always eastward,
everything behind them
weightless
and surely in white.

And their Scotch or Irish boy,
or even Maronite,
will be clean and kind and work hard
in a tyre-bay or whatever,
build an extension,
make a good life,
and the girls would sit together here
pacifico
pacifico
watching their grandsons
catch the wave below.

This had Gaitano dreamed,
and kept dreaming,
lying beside them
each night,
hands still creased
with engine oil,
the ocean revolving down there
as he learned quarter by quarter
all the southern stars
until he died in English:

Father of the above
and beloved husband of Jessie Palise
who died 31 October 1936
aged 49

leaving incised
through weather and all time

Eterni Angelette
del nostro cuore
nostre figlie

'War Poems': Six Pieces

'The dead are unhappy enough as they are.
Is it necessary to dedicate laments to them forever?'

1 PRELUDE (for mouth organ)

suck blow   suck blow   suck blow

when whippoorwills call

suck blow   suck blow   suck blow

and evening is nigh

suck blow   suck blow   suck blow

I'll meet you in my

suck blow   suck blow   suck blow

blow   blue heav - en

then heeled himself over   the bolster taking

the print of his cheek   and all the rest

lay down beside   knowing there would be dreams

and that none would ever   see again

their own folk   or their borough streets

and walk out at night   but hoped fortune

would find where they fell   and see them carried

into the earth   narrowed for their cot

and carried thus   into the earth

and that a porch would be raised   and a cup put by

that would gleam in the soil   as at the feast of life

when the burnisher lit   the night with his work

the reed sang   and there was plum and nectarine

May their trees   nod by that place

as long as there is time   between dark and dark

(after *Beowulf*)

3   PERSONAL EFFECTS (O sole mio)
    The Soldiers' Cemetery, Orvieto

Ti amo.

Perhaps he does. And she him.
They've chalked it on the wall.
In ten years maybe they will be passing here to take
Their children to some treat or due solemnity
And smile sidelong as they pass.

For now, their condom, still heavy enough
Not to blow across the troopers' graves,
Lies here as some part of their story,
Maybe its closure . . . – *Ciao* – *Ciao* . . .
Beginning to perish across this lawn
Of splayed, parted or contorted boys
Who winked and grinned as well as died.

49

4   SOVIET POET READING (Words without Music)

This poet wears his laurels in his face.

Held together at the dressing-station,
under these lights it looks waxy,
mastic-yellow where it was built back
almost from the skull into the new man.

It will not move so much,
but the mouth will open
and would sing just for comrades,
the black dolls
of the KV cupola.

This poet wears his laurels in his face
but critically that cannot be –
his metres serve him, them, now us,
and he must not go
unsuspected.

We scrutators
of his lines and countenance
snigger or sneeze
sneeze or snigger.

5   THAT ROOM   THAT SEA (Abide with me)

I remember her white hair and her smiling
no one to be afraid of there   no uneasiness
through the dark afternoons alongside the snow-field
of her counterpane and pillows   save her bosom
and the steaming of the mighty poultices the blue nurse prepared
pink ointment plastered across a rug of lint
the pain it must be   but she has to   'Go out now'

No one to be afraid of   but mauve drapes heavily held
she had been mad   I didn't know
locked up for a while
some buses turn off and go round that way
I was on one once   Who is this man
speaking to me suddenly with apron pan and spatula?

He was not from there   he is gone now
probably forever   the deep mauves and the window
on to what seems to be no outside
How could she smile so much?   when she had been nothing
and he name rank and serial number   dysenteric
jam-packed in the prison-ship   the listing of her mind
her son roughly wrapped   brokenly spoken over
by whoever knew something of the words

6   SALVAGE (Coda . . .)

What happened
to the despised bristly khaki,
the battledress

of lancejack
humiliation and homesickness?
– Got rid of.

The old kit-bag
hung behind the door for years
for salvage:

paper and tins –
no ashes, egg-shells, no vegetable
matter.

On a waiting bus
one night – Cold Meece, the back-of-beyond,
by the R.O.F. gate –

the engine ticking down,
the reflections from the sparse bulbs
inscrutable,

out there in the
unseeable dark, already emplaced
in the soft fields,

the war came back,
coming in overhead, not with its flame
or clamour,

but its assumption,
its passage through walls, its filling
of the heart

52

so it can take
these souls, their nearest, dearest, their
hallway lights,

curtain pelmets,
non-drip gloss, chrysanthemums, new divans,
the D.I.Y.

of happiness,
of yearned-for, precious, modern life,
all

into oil-smoke,
polder, snow-drift, tideway,
notification.

That was a
future as it turned out; not this,
as it has

turned out, luckily,
and not exactly here, where my mind
can shake itself

as I remember
the bus start up and its lights
sweep the fields.

Nothing there,
some paper, plastic, brown glass,
green glass, clear glass.

53